FIRST GRAPHICS

MY COMMUNITY

A VISIT TO THE VET

BY LORI MORTENSEN

ILLUSTRATED BY JEFFREY THOMPSON

Consultant: Jennifer Zablotny, DVM
Member, American Veterinary Medical Association

CAPSTONE PRESS
a capstone imprint

First Graphics are published by Capstone Press,
151 Good Counsel Drive, P.O. Box 669, Mankato, Minnesota 56002.
www.capstonepub.com

Printed in the United States of America in Stevens Point, Wisconsin.

032010
005741WZF10

Books published by Capstone Press are manufactured with paper containing at least 10 percent post-consumer waste.

Library of Congress Cataloging-in-Publication Data

Mortensen, Lori.
A visit to the vet / by Lori Mortensen; illustrated by Jeffrey Thompson.
p. cm.—(First graphics. My community)
Includes bibliographical references and index.
Summary: "In graphic novel format, text and illustrations describes a visit to the veterinarian"—Provided by publisher.
ISBN 978-1-4296-4509-6 (library binding)
ISBN 978-1-4296-5614-6 (paperback)
1. Veterinarians—Juvenile literature. 2. Veterinary medicine—Vocational guidance—Juvenile literature. I. Title. II. Series.
SF756.M67 2011
636.089092—dc22
2009051474

Editor: **Erika L. Shores**
Designer: **Alison Thiele**
Art Director: **Nathan Gassman**
Production Specialist: **Laura Manthe**

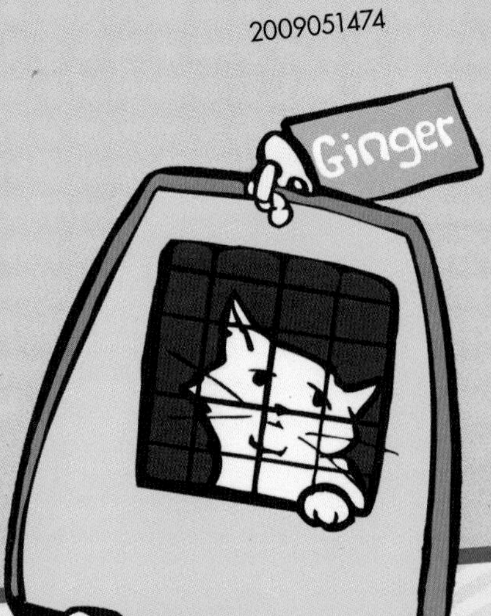
Ginger

TABLE OF CONTENTS

Pet Check

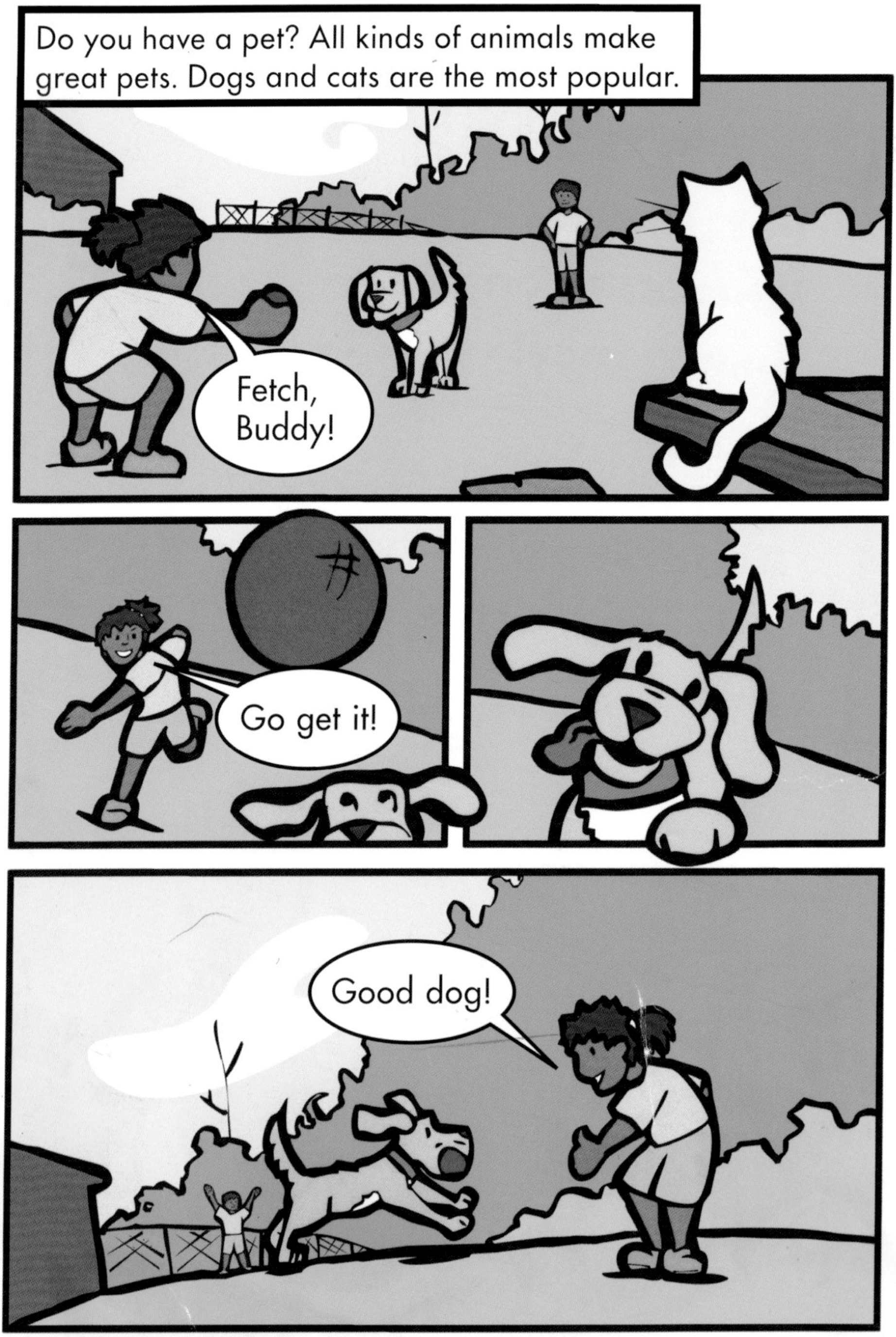

Do you have a pet? All kinds of animals make great pets. Dogs and cats are the most popular.
Fetch, Buddy!
Go get it!
Good dog!

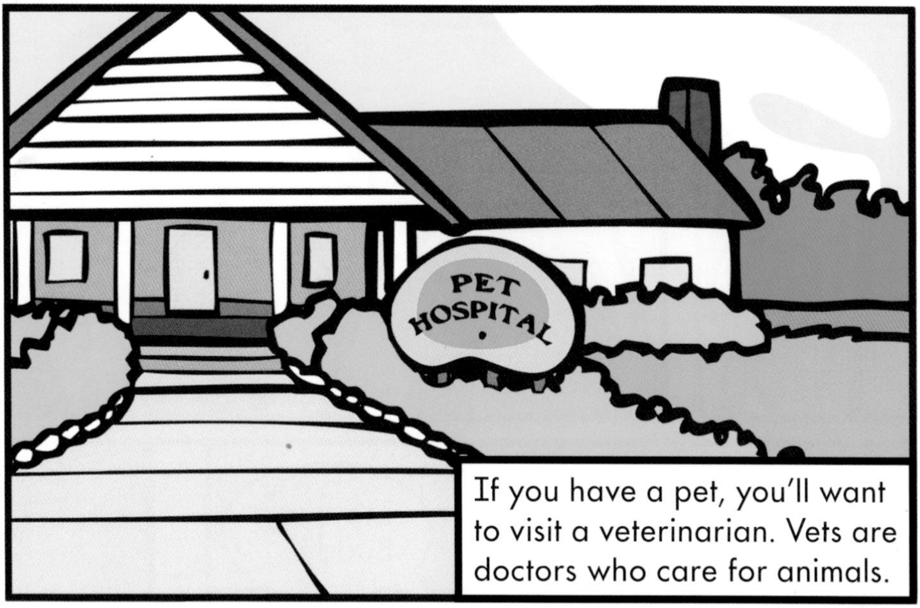
PET HOSPITAL
If you have a pet, you'll want to visit a veterinarian. Vets are doctors who care for animals.

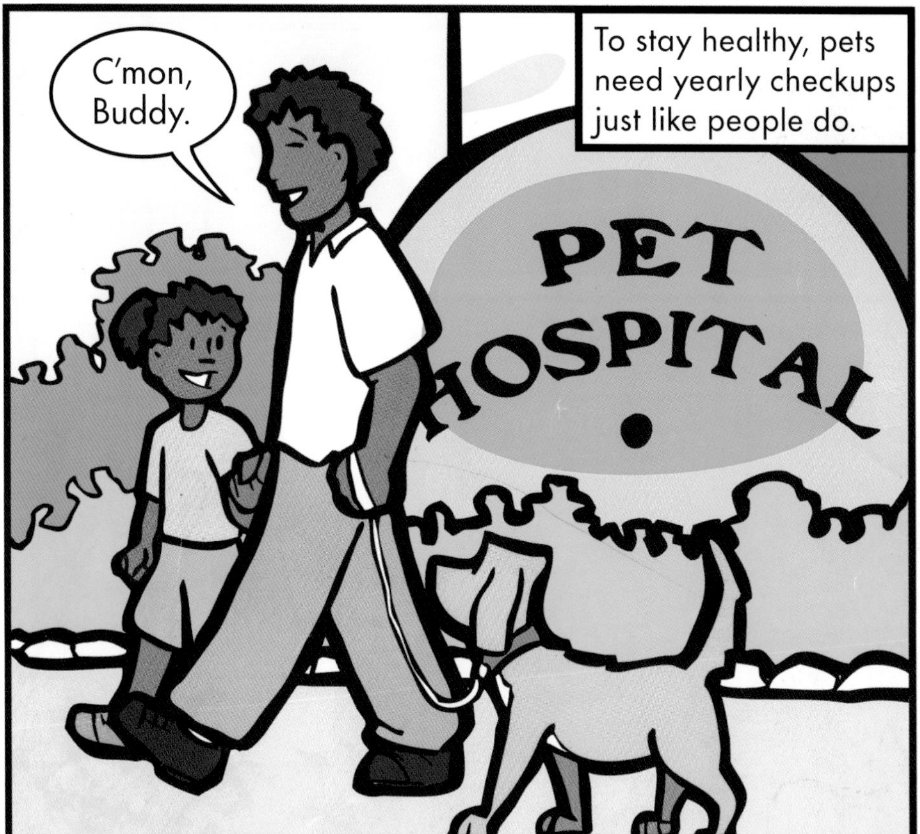
C'mon, Buddy.
To stay healthy, pets need yearly checkups just like people do.
PET HOSPITAL

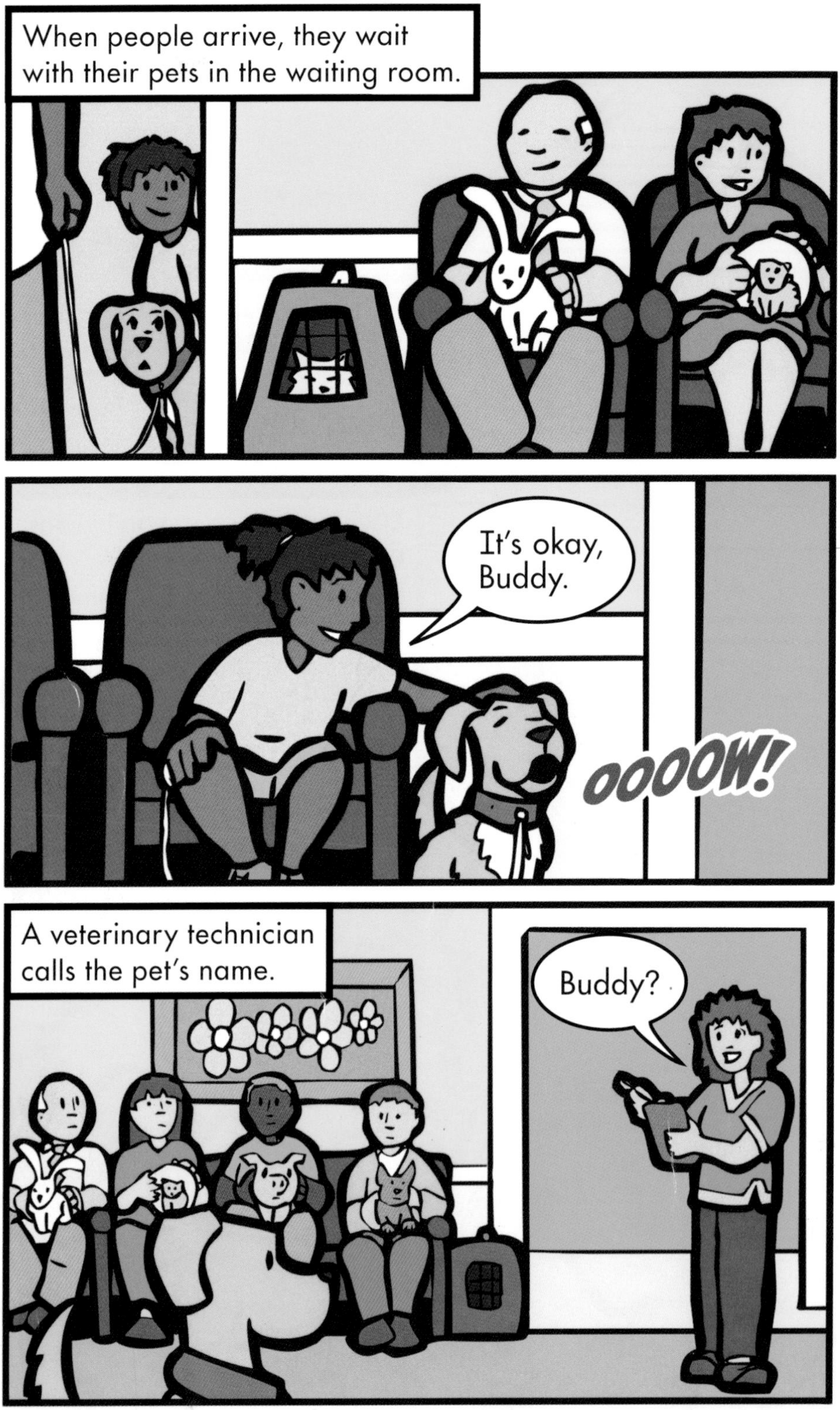
When people arrive, they wait with their pets in the waiting room.
It's okay, Buddy.
OOOOW!
A veterinary technician calls the pet's name.
Buddy?

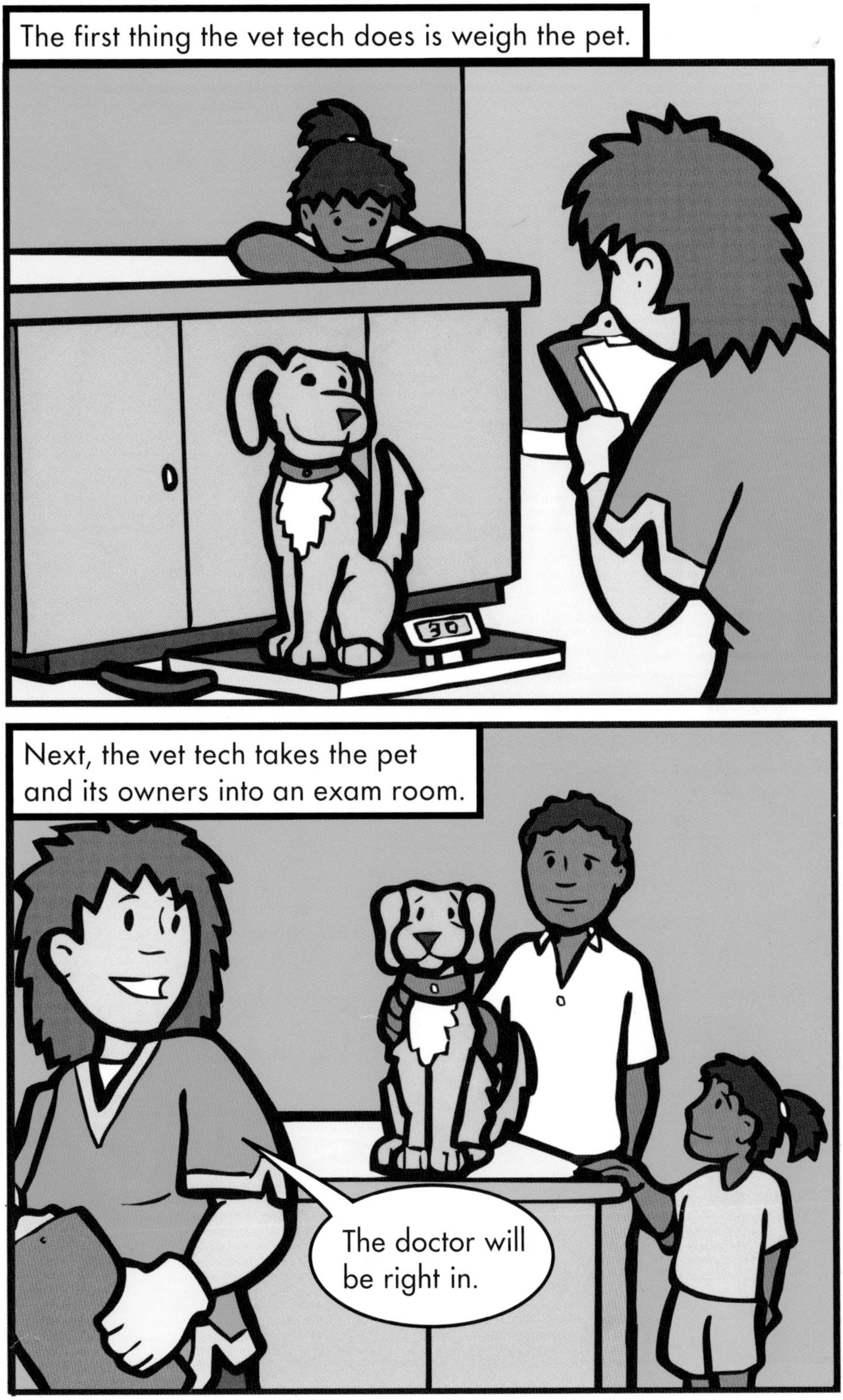
The first thing the vet tech does is weigh the pet.
30
Next, the vet tech takes the pet and its owners into an exam room.
The doctor will be right in.

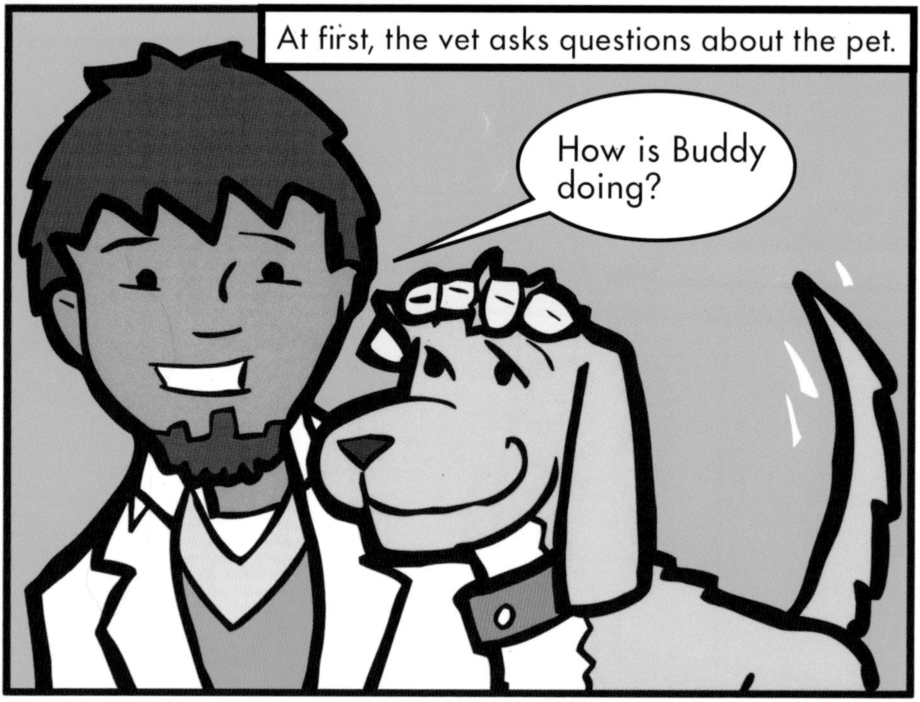
At first, the vet asks questions about the pet.
How is Buddy doing?

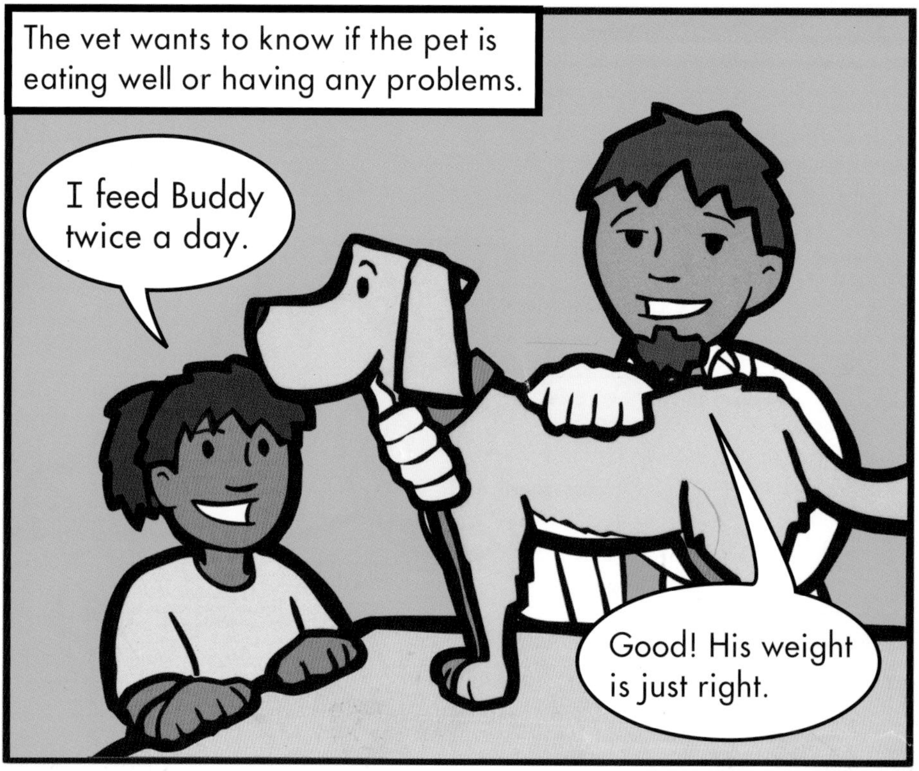
The vet wants to know if the pet is eating well or having any problems.
I feed Buddy twice a day.
Good! His weight is just right.

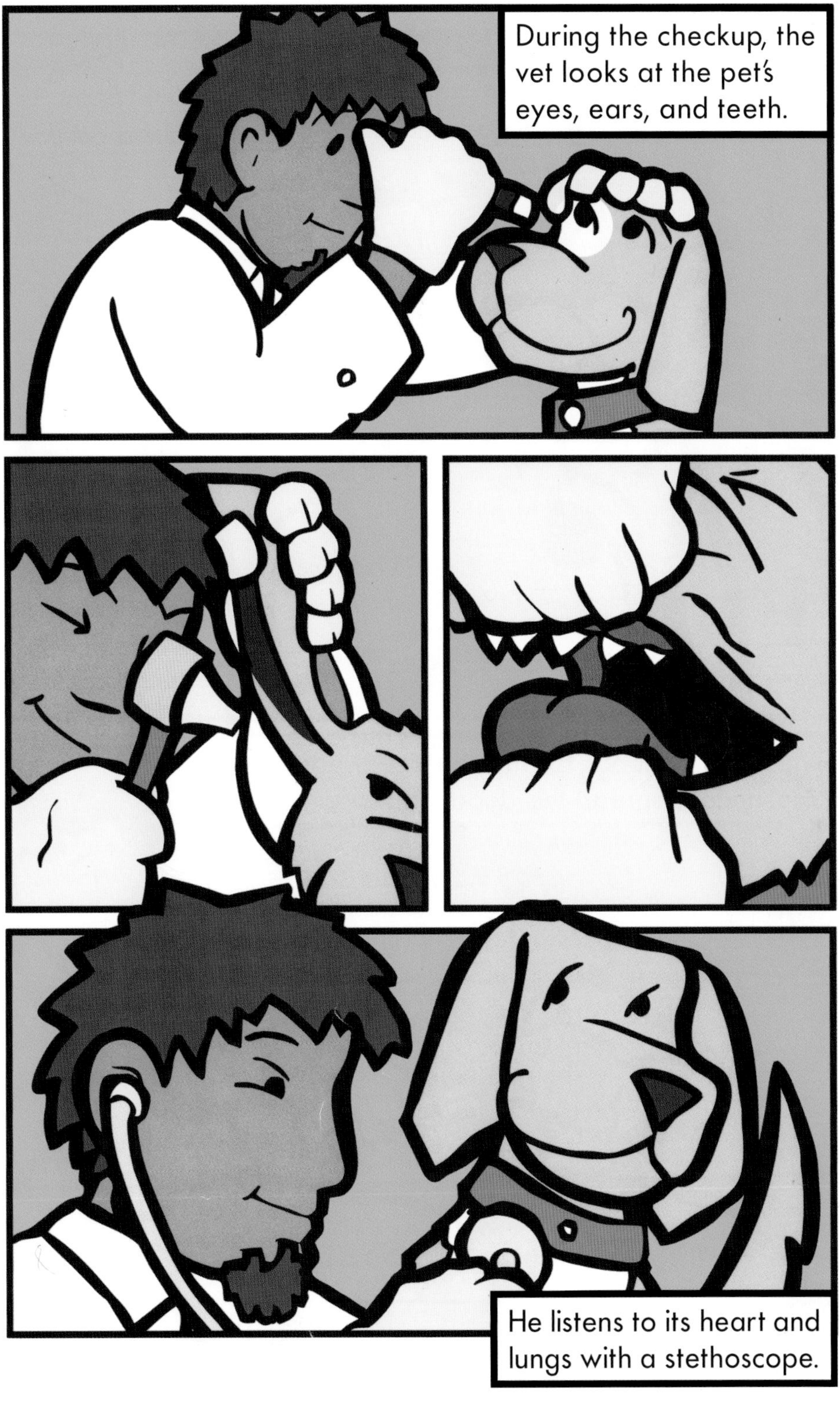
During the checkup, the vet looks at the pet's eyes, ears, and teeth.
He listens to its heart and lungs with a stethoscope.

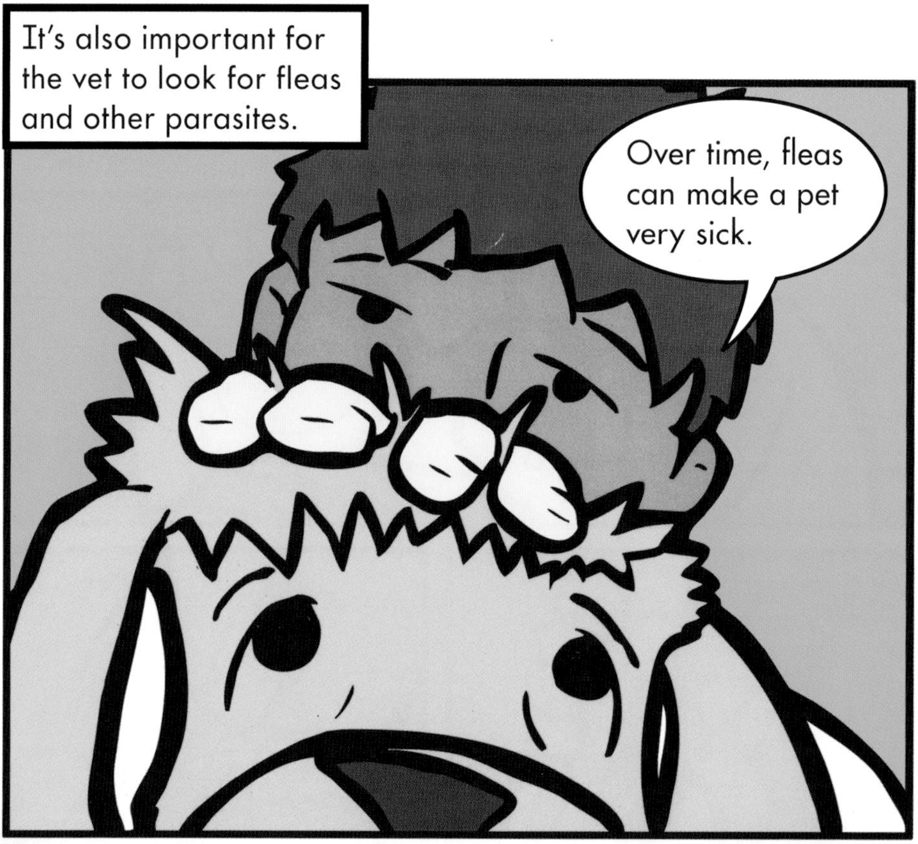
It's also important for the vet to look for fleas and other parasites.
Over time, fleas can make a pet very sick.

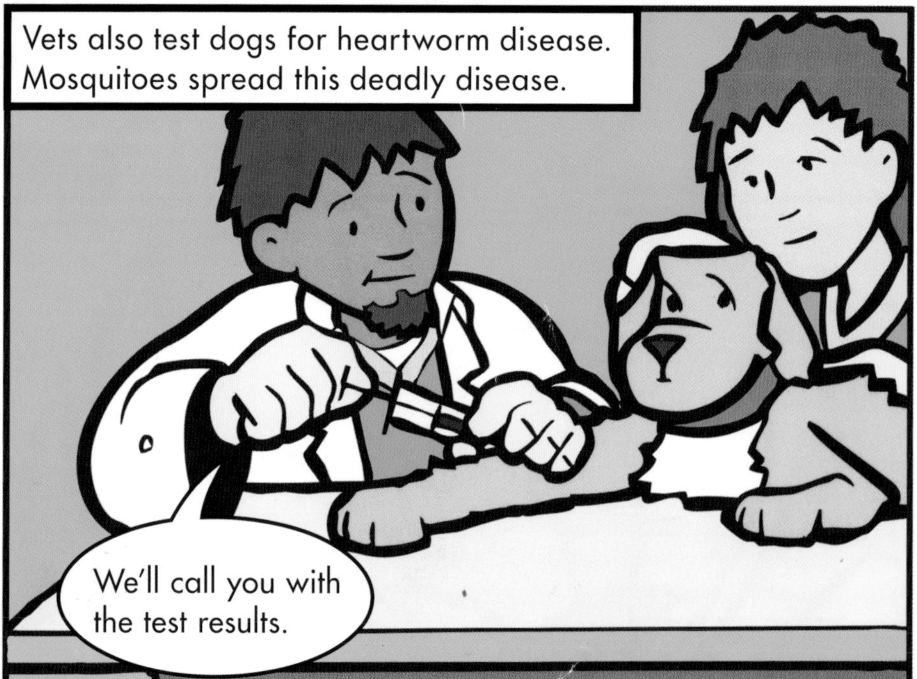
Vets also test dogs for heartworm disease. Mosquitoes spread this deadly disease.
We'll call you with the test results.

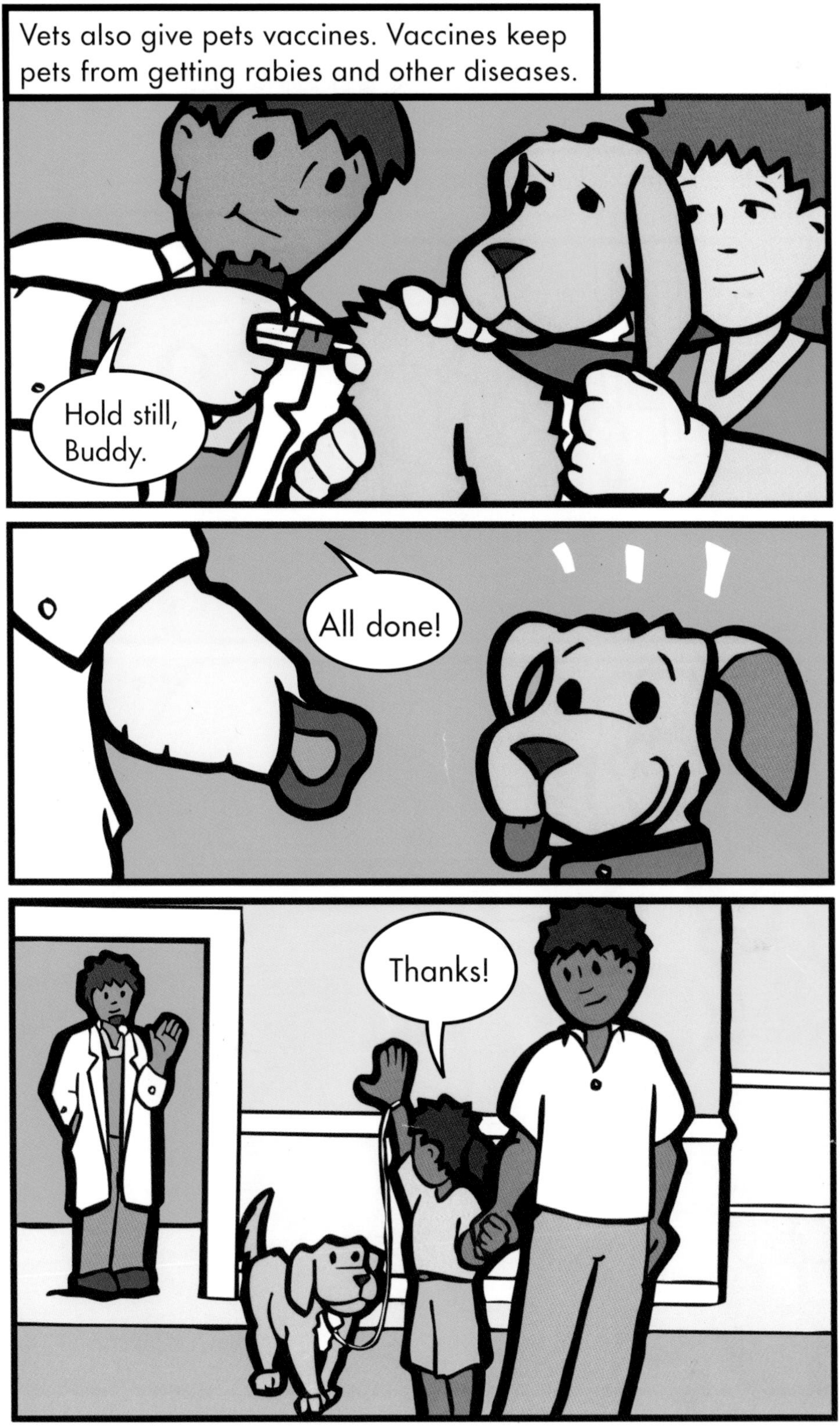
Vets also give pets vaccines. Vaccines keep pets from getting rabies and other diseases.
Hold still, Buddy.
All done!
Thanks!

WHAT'S WRONG?

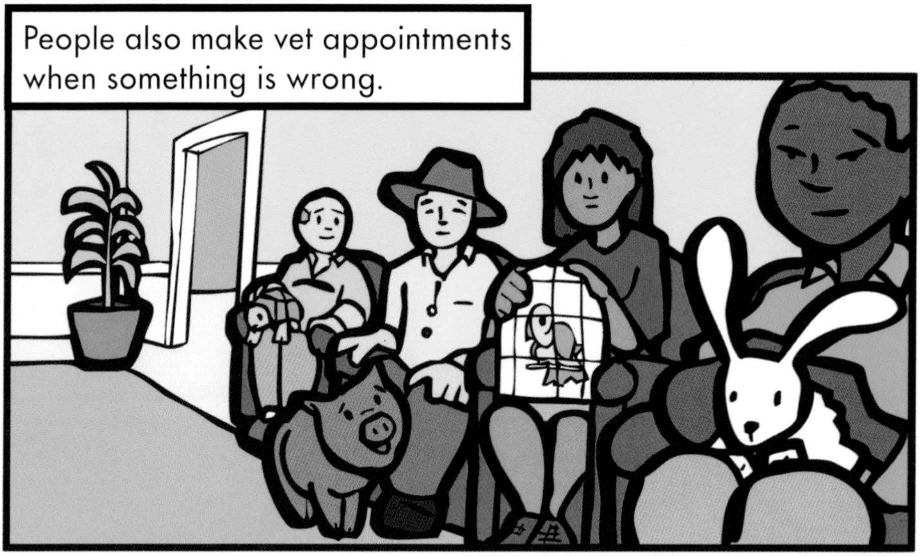
People also make vet appointments when something is wrong.

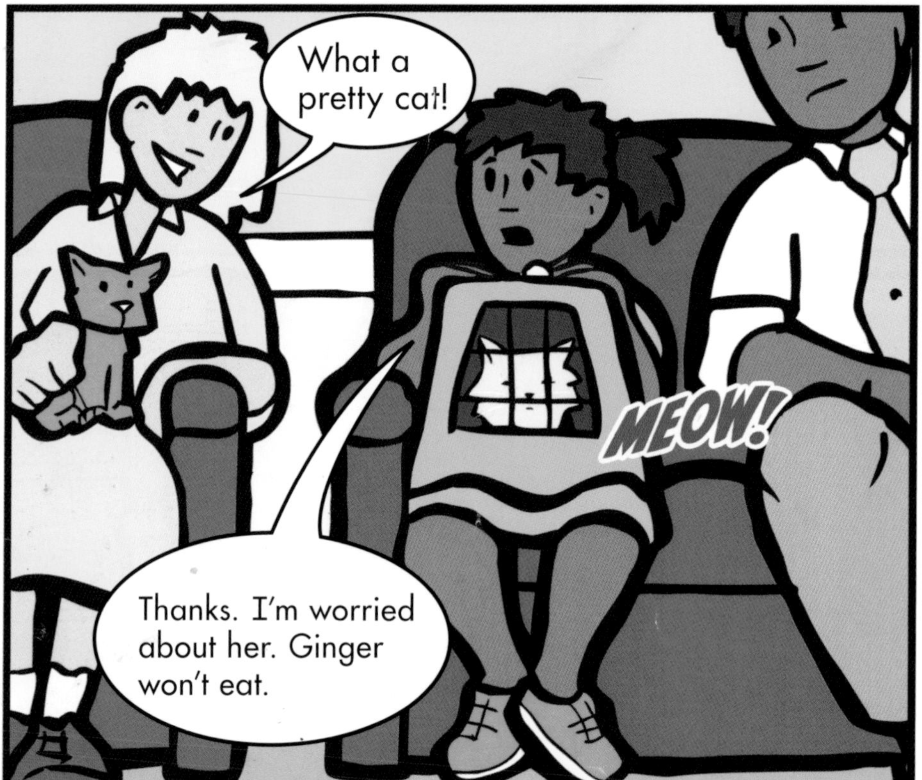
What a pretty cat!
Thanks. I'm worried about her. Ginger won't eat.
MEOW!

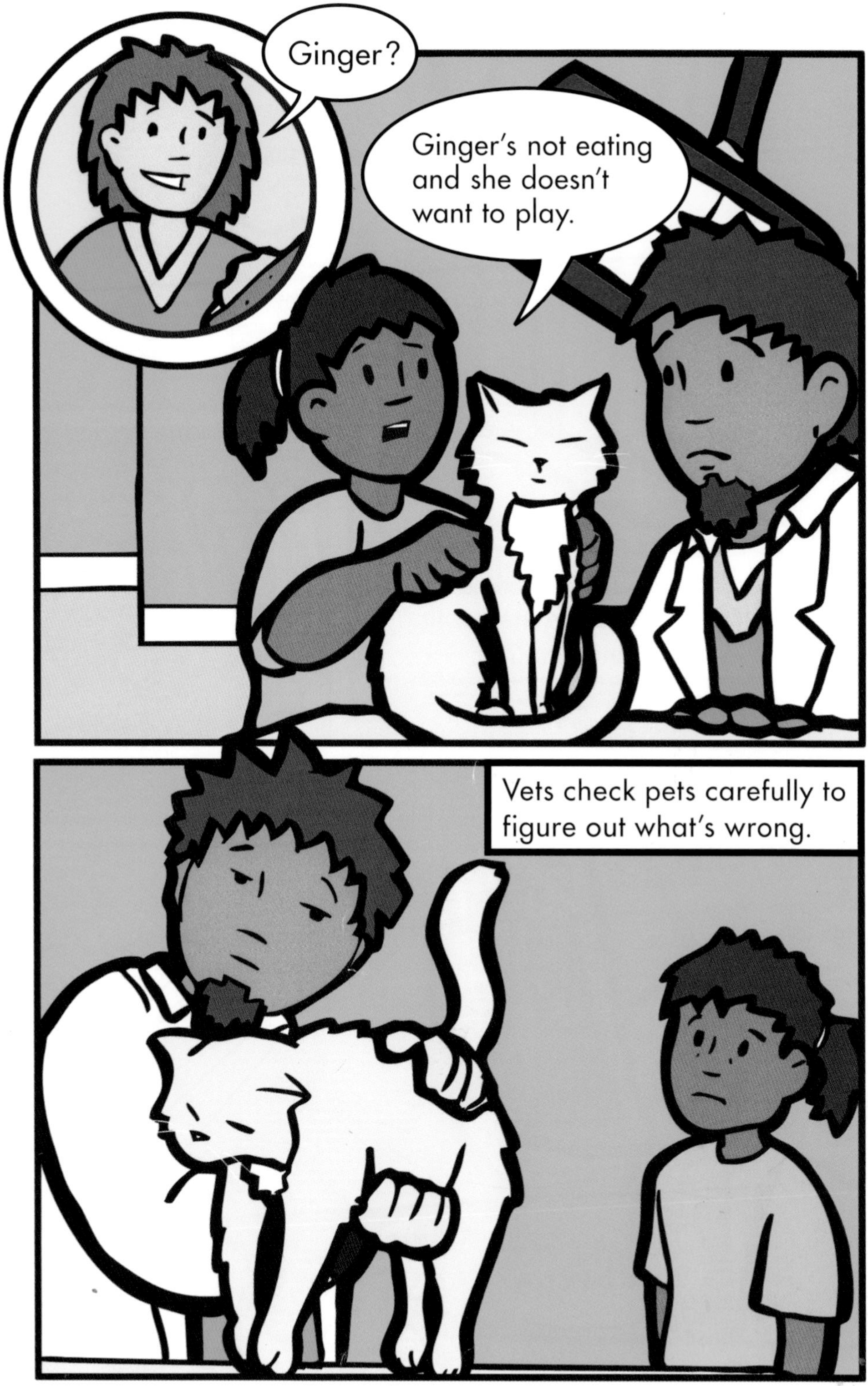
Ginger?
Ginger's not eating and she doesn't want to play.
Vets check pets carefully to figure out what's wrong.

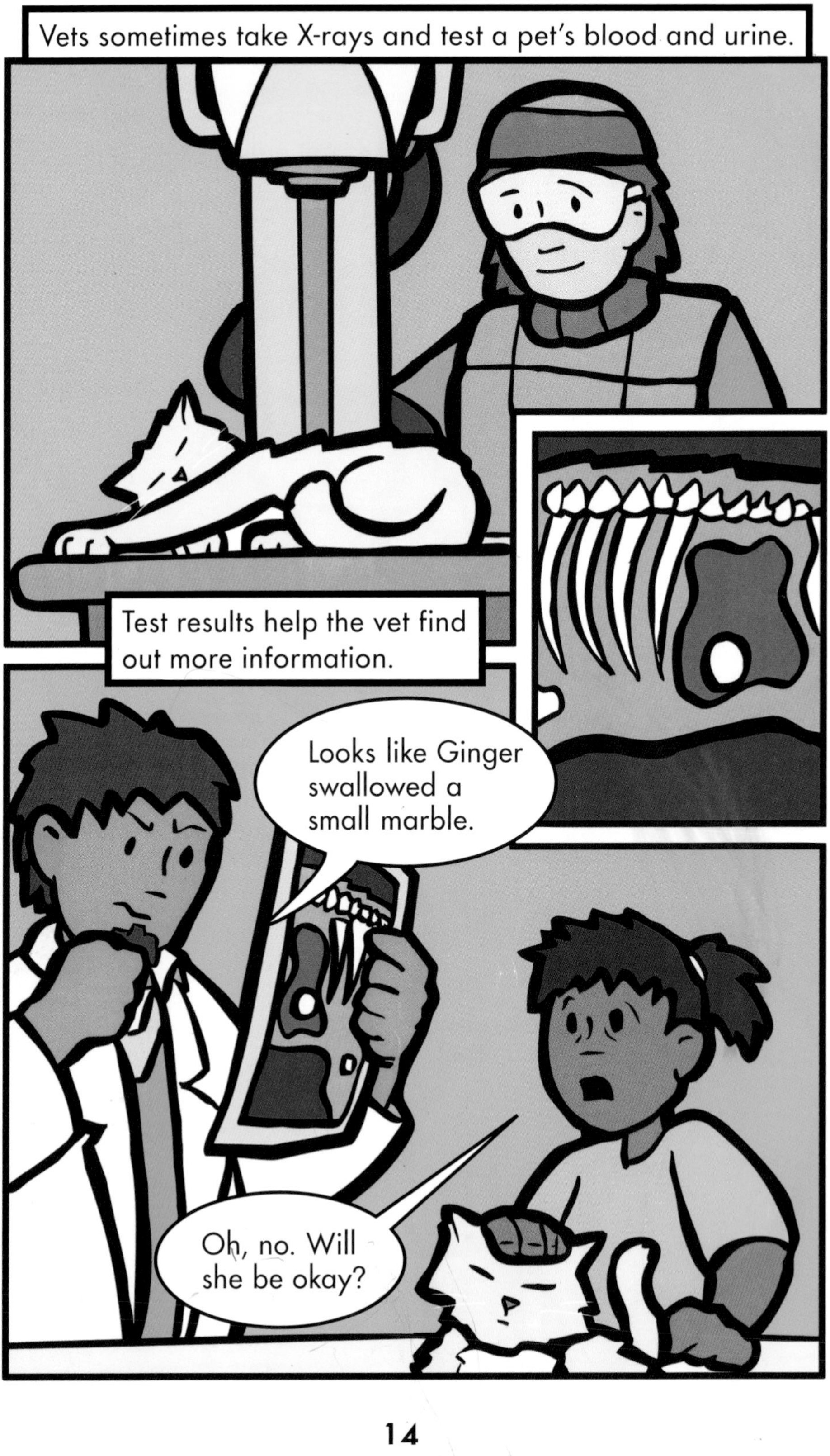
Vets sometimes take X-rays and test a pet's blood and urine.
Test results help the vet find out more information.
Looks like Ginger swallowed a small marble.
Oh, no. Will she be okay?

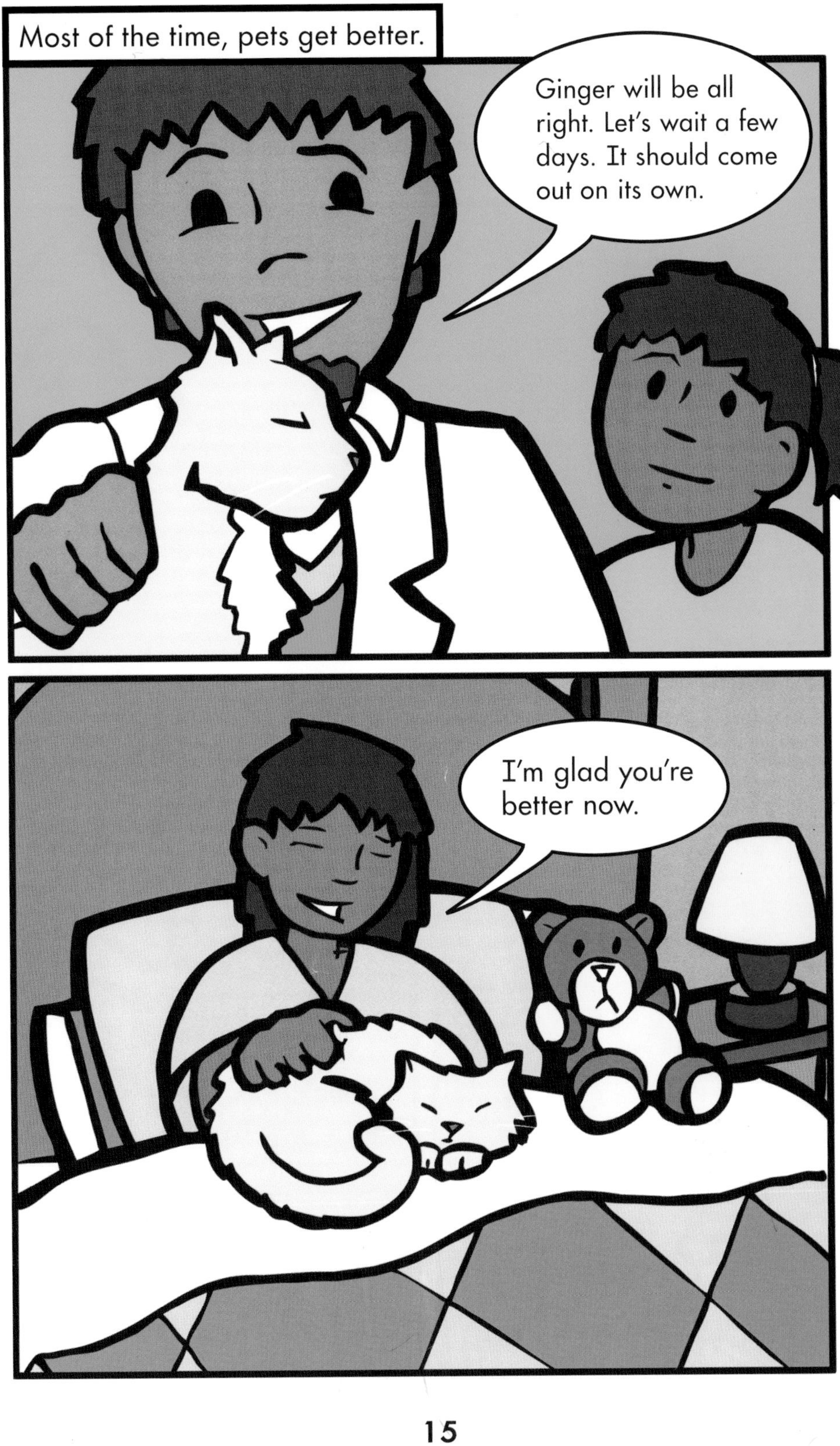
Most of the time, pets get better.
Ginger will be all right. Let's wait a few days. It should come out on its own.
I'm glad you're better now.

EMERGENCY!

Sometimes pets have accidents and injuries just like people do. The pet will need treatment quickly.

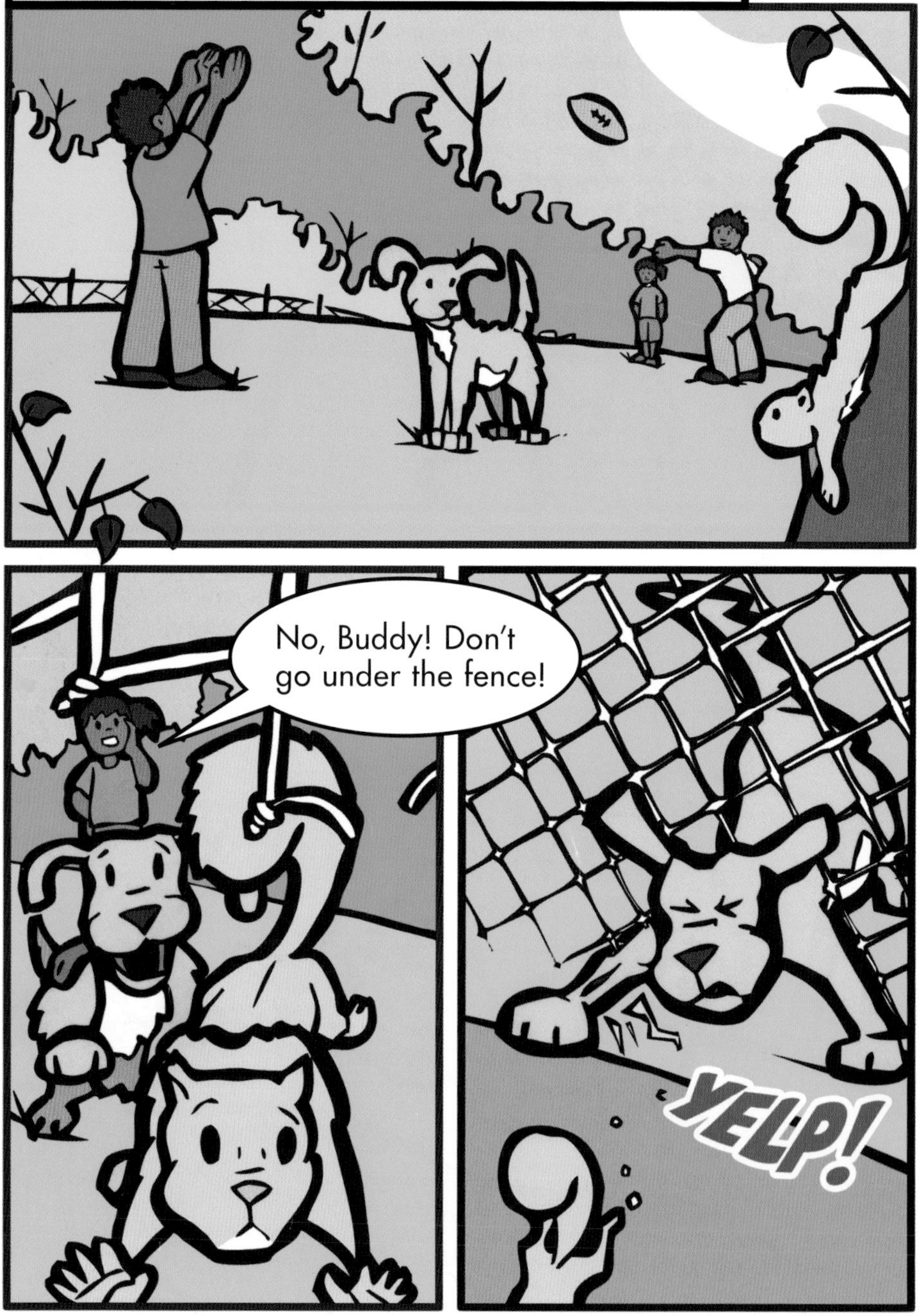
No, Buddy! Don't go under the fence!
YELP!

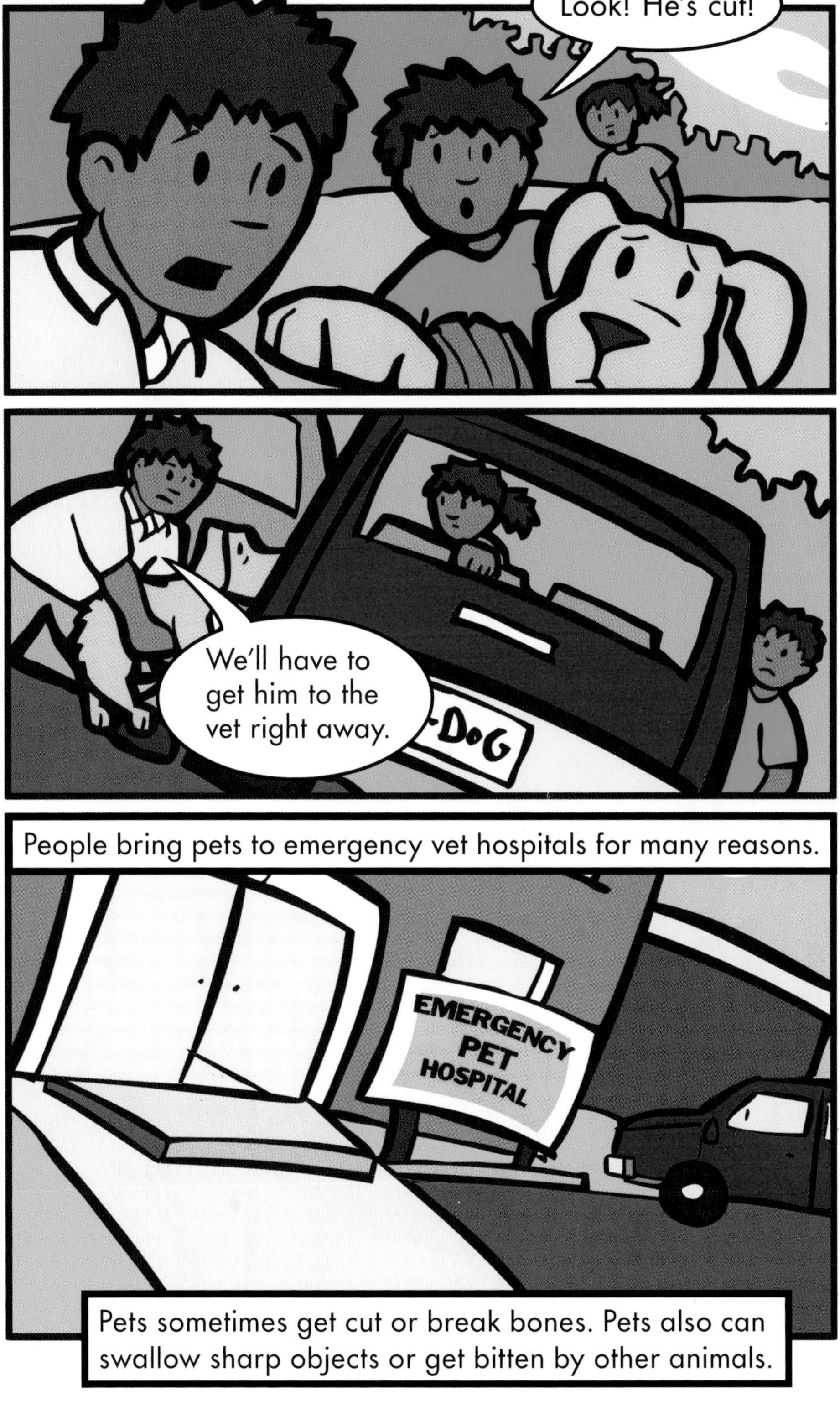
Look! He's cut!
We'll have to get him to the vet right away.
-DOG
People bring pets to emergency vet hospitals for many reasons.
EMERGENCY PET HOSPITAL
Pets sometimes get cut or break bones. Pets also can swallow sharp objects or get bitten by other animals.

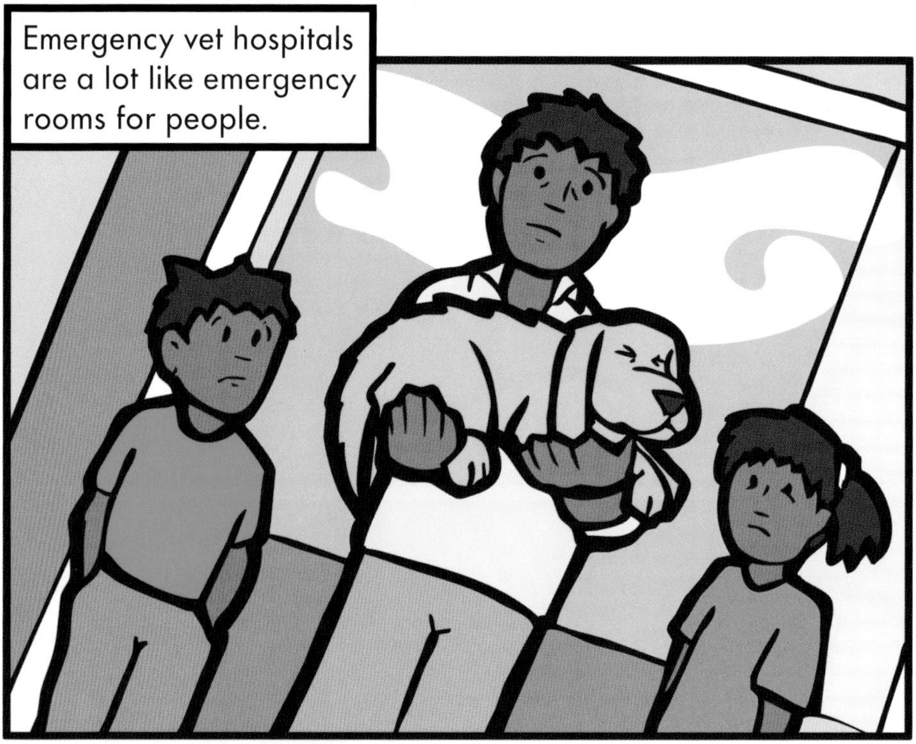
Emergency vet hospitals are a lot like emergency rooms for people.

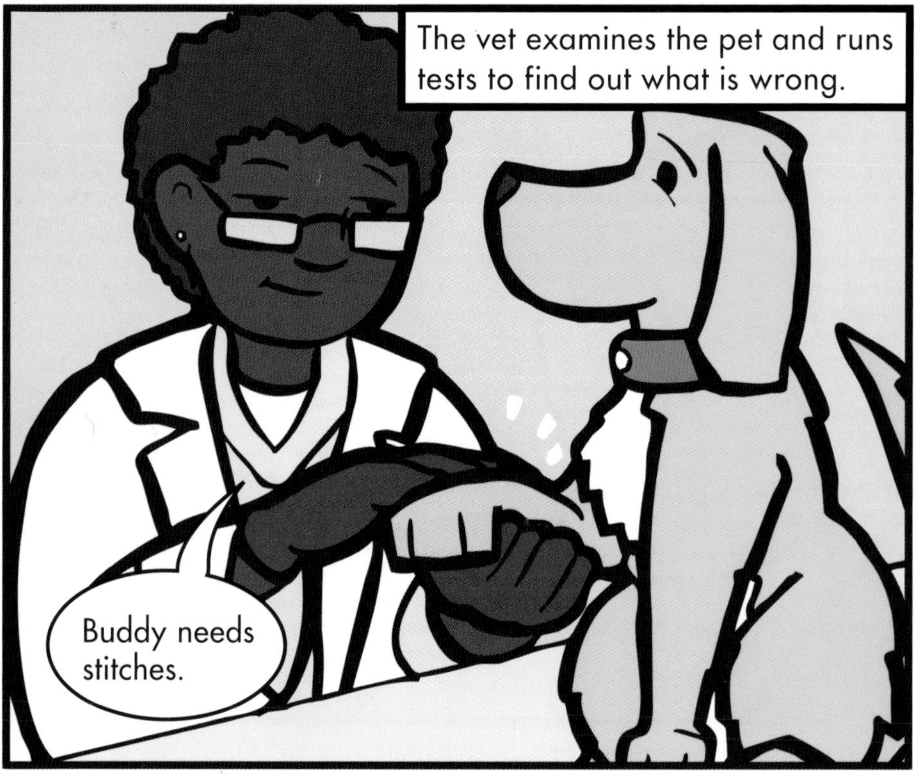
The vet examines the pet and runs tests to find out what is wrong.
Buddy needs stitches.

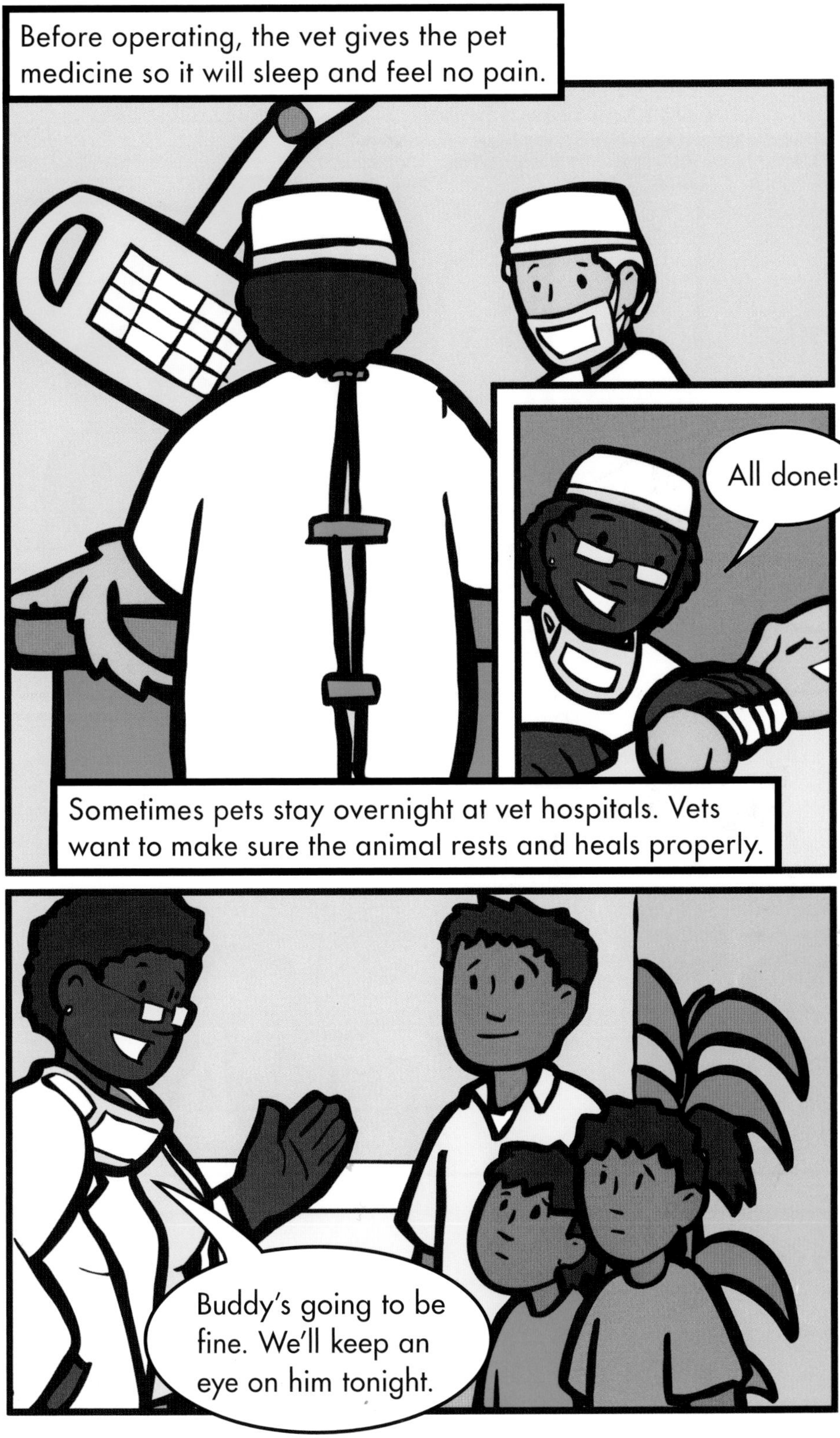
Before operating, the vet gives the pet medicine so it will sleep and feel no pain.
All done!
Sometimes pets stay overnight at vet hospitals. Vets want to make sure the animal rests and heals properly.
Buddy's going to be fine. We'll keep an eye on him tonight.

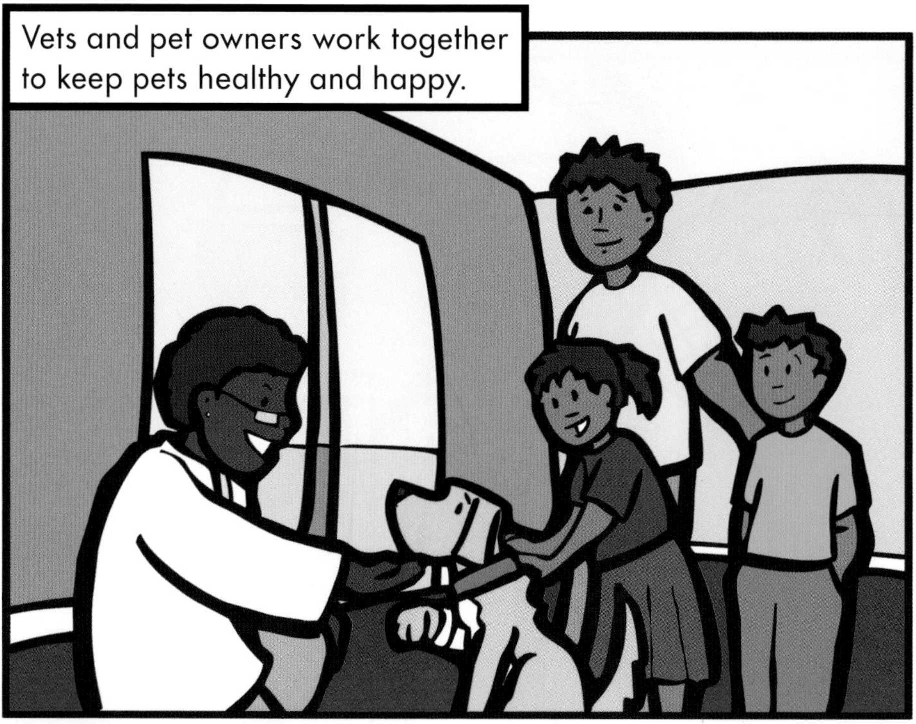
Vets and pet owners work together to keep pets healthy and happy.

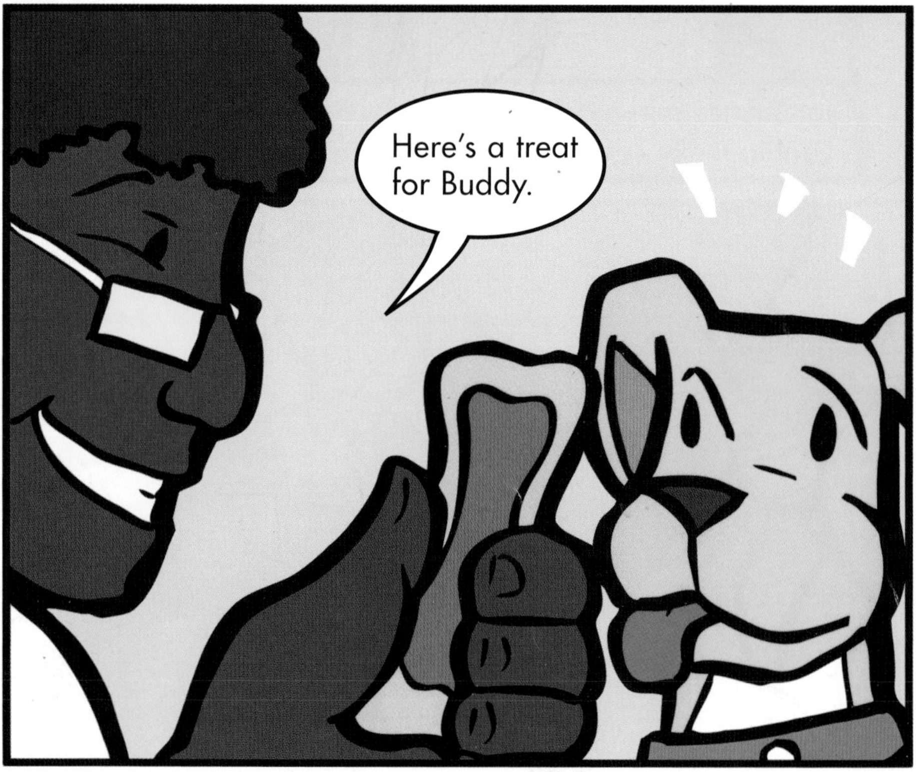
Here's a treat for Buddy.

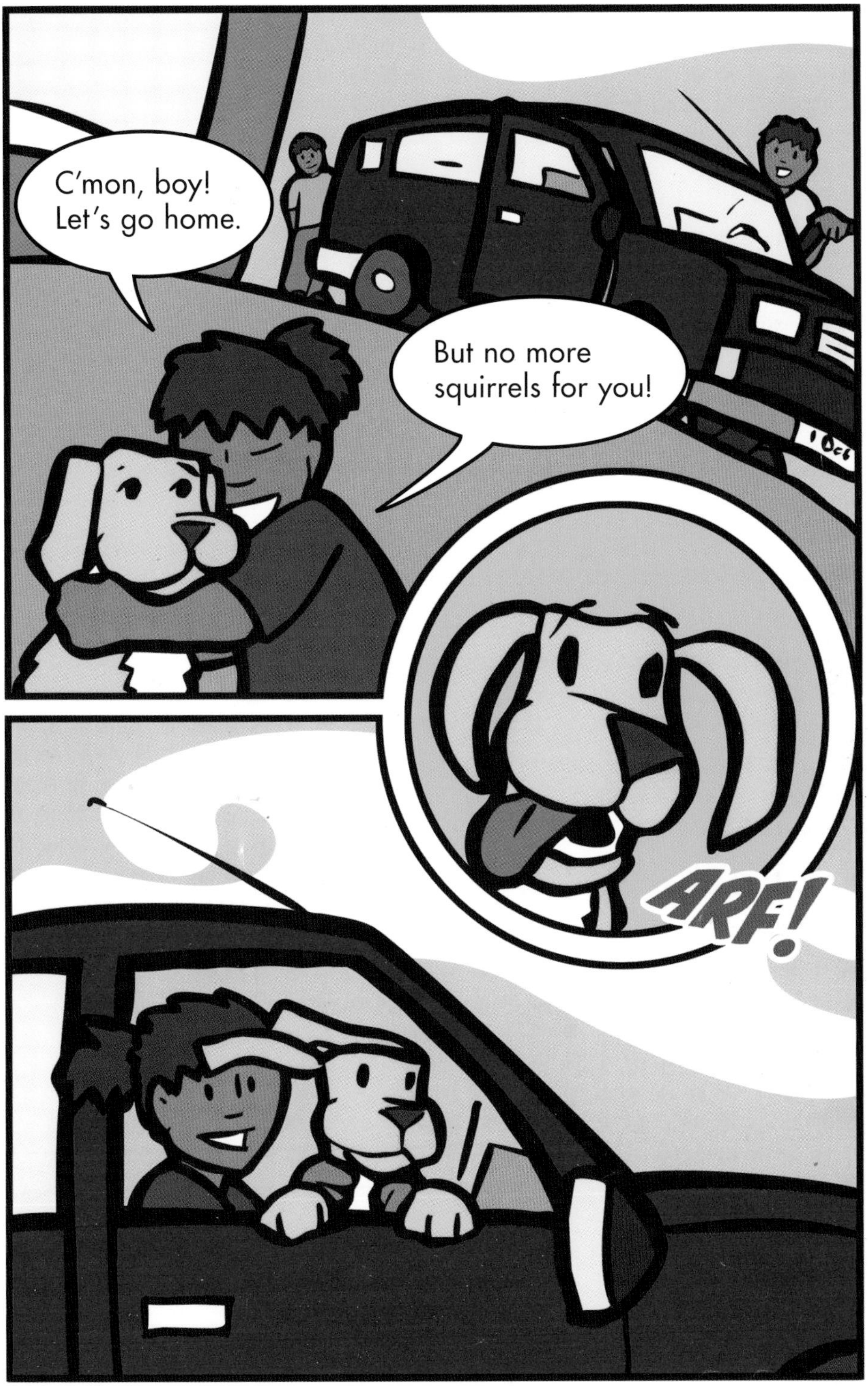
C'mon, boy! Let's go home.
But no more squirrels for you!
ARF!

GLOSSARY

heartworm—a disease that dogs can get from mosquitoes; heartworm disease can be deadly if left untreated

parasite—an animal or plant that needs to live on or inside another animal or plant to survive

rabies—a deadly disease that people and animals can get from the bite of an animal with the disease

stethoscope—a tool used by a doctor to listen to the heart and lungs

stitch—a thread used to close up a wound

urine—a person's or an animal's liquid waste

vaccine—medicine given to prevent a disease

veterinarian technician—a person trained to help a veterinarian

X-ray—a photograph that shows bones inside the body

READ MORE

Bennett, Leonie. *A Day with Animal Doctors.*
I Love Reading. New York: Bearport Publishing,
2006.

Kalman, Bobbie. *Help Keep Animals Healthy.*
My Community and Its Helpers. New York:
Crabtree, 2005.

Rau, Dana Meachen. *Veterinarian.* Benchmark
Rebus. New York: Marshall Cavendish Benchmark,
2008.

INTERNET SITES

FactHound offers a safe, fun way to find Internet
sites related to this book. All of the sites on
FactHound have been researched by our staff.

Here's all you do:

Visit *www.facthound.com*

FactHound will fetch the best sites for you!

INDEX

My Community

Titles in this set:

A Day at the Fire Station

Going to the Dentist

A Visit to the Vet

Working on the Farm

First Graphics